Nell picks a cat hat.

Tess picks a cat hat.

Tess packs a red bag.

Nell packs a red bag.

Nell has a big bell.

Tess has no big bell.

Tess gets off and tuts.

Nell huffs and puffs.

Huff!

Tess is up a hill.

Tess is in a mess.

Nell can get Tess up.

Nell is in a mess!

/l/

:paw: After reading :paw:

Letters and Sounds: Phase 2

Word count: 60

Focus phonemes: /l/, ll, ss

Common exception words: is, and, no, has

Curriculum links: Understanding the World: People and Communities; The World

Early learning goals: Reading: read and understand simple sentences; use phonic knowledge to decode regular words and read them aloud accurately; read some common irregular words; demonstrate understanding when talking with others about what they have read

Developing fluency

- Encourage your child to sound talk and then blend the words, e.g. m/e/ss. It may help to point to each sound as your child reads.
- Then ask your child to reread the sentence to support fluency and understanding.
- You could reread the whole book to your child to model fluency and rhythm in the story.

Phonic practice

- Ask your child to sound talk and blend each of the following words: h/u/ff, m/e/ss, p/a/ck/s, p/i/ck/s.
- Can you match the rhyming words? **bell, Tess, huffs, puffs, Nell, mess**. (*bell/Nell, Tess/mess, huff/puff*)
- Look at the "I spy sounds" pages (14–15). Discuss the picture with your child. Can they find items/ examples of words with the /l/ and "ll" sounds? (*lion, laugh, leaf, leaves, lemon, lemonade, log, lock, doll, roll, fill, ball*)

Extending vocabulary

- Ask your child:
  - On pages 2–3 Nell and Tess pick a cat hat. What different types of hats can you think of? (e.g. *pirate hat, cowboy hat, top hat, baseball cap, sun hat, helmet, chef's hat*)
  - On page 8, Tess is cross. Can you think of other words that mean cross? (e.g. *mad, angry, annoyed, furious*)